DATE DUE

DEMCO 38-296

John R. Pierce: Pioneer in Satellite Communications

Jim Whiting

Mitchell Lane
PUBLISHERS

PO Box 196 • Hockessin, Delaware 19707
www.mitchelllane.com

Unlocking the Secrets of Science

Profiling 20th Century Achievers in Science, Medicine, and Technology

John R. Pierce: Pioneer in Satellite Communications

Printing   1   2   3   4   5   6   7   8   9   10

Library of Congress Cataloging-in-Publication Data
Whiting, Jim, 1943-
    John R. Pierce: pioneer in satellite communications/Jim Whiting.
       p. cm. — (Unlocking the secrets of science)
    Summary: A biography of the engineer who designed and helped launch the first communications satellite, Telstar, and who developed new uses for satellite communications, paving the way for the cordless telephone, cell phone, and wireless headsets.
    ISBN 1-58415-205-2 (Library Bound)
    1. Pierce, John Robinson, 1910—Juvenile literature. 2. Telecommunications engineers—United States—Biography—Juvenile literature. 3. Artificial satellites in telecommunication—History—Juvenile literature. [1. Pierce, John Robinson, 1910- 2. Telecommunications engineers. 3. Artificial satellites in communication.] I. Title. II. Unlocking the secrets of science.
    TK5102.56.P54W49 2003
    621.382'092—dc22   2003021306

ABOUT THE AUTHOR: Jim Whiting has been a journalist, writer, editor, and photographer for more than 20 years. In addition to a lengthy stint as publisher of *Northwest Runner* magazine, Mr. Whiting has contributed to the *Seattle Times*, *Conde Nast Traveler*, *Newsday*, and *Saturday Evening Post*. He has edited more than 40 titles in the Mitchell Lane Real-Life Reader Biography series and Unlocking the Secrets of Science. He lives in Washington state with his wife and two teenage sons.

PHOTO CREDITS: cover: Bell Laboratories; p. 6 Hulton/Archive; p. 11 Corbis; p. 14 Bell Laboratories; p. 18 California Institute of Technology; p. 24 Lucent; p. 29 Lucent; p. 30 AP Photos; p. 36 Lucent.

PUBLISHER'S NOTE: In selecting those persons to be profiled in this series, we first attempted to identify the most notable accomplishments of the 20th century in science, medicine, and technology. When we were done, we noted a serious deficiency in the inclusion of women. For the greater part of the 20th century science, medicine, and technology were male-dominated fields. In many cases, the contributions of women went unrecognized. Women have tried for years to be included in these areas, and in many cases, women worked side by side with men who took credit for their ideas and discoveries. Even as we move forward into the 21st century, we find women still sadly underrepresented. It is not an oversight, therefore, that we profiled mostly male achievers. Information simply does not exist to include a fair selection of women.

Contents

H.G. Wells (1866-1946) was an English author who published several science fiction novels. His most famous works were The Time Machine *and* The War of the Worlds. *He also wrote* The Island of Dr. Moreau, The Invisible Man *and* The First Man in the Moon.

Chapter 1

A Nightmare Sparks a Dream

On the afternoon of June 13, 1944, the citizens of London, England, were feeling pretty good about the way that World War II was going. Thousands of American, British and Canadian troops had splashed ashore on the Normandy coast of German-occupied France the week before. Many thought that the end of the conflict was finally in sight. It had been several years since the Blitz, the horrible nine-month period in 1940 and 1941 when London had endured almost nightly bombings by German aircraft. Huge fires and crumbling buildings became everyday sights. More than 30,000 people were killed and another 50,000 wounded before the attacks ended. Since then, the Germans had left the city alone.

That was about to change on this warm spring day. People on the streets suddenly heard a strange buzzing overhead. They looked up, trying to spot whatever was making the odd noise. Abruptly the sound ceased. Moments later there was a huge explosion.

That day marked the beginning of Nazi Germany's final onslaught against the British capital. German scientists had developed the V-1, a device whose name came from the German word *Vergeltungswaffe*, or "revenge weapon." Resembling a small airplane and propelled by a jet engine, it was launched from catapults in occupied Holland. The pilotless V-1s would rise to an altitude of 3,000 feet and attain a speed of up to 350 miles per hour. At a predetermined point, the engine would stop. With its power cut off, the V-1 would plunge toward the ground. Nearly a ton of high explosives would detonate when it crashed.

These "buzz bombs," as they were nicknamed, quickly became all too familiar. Up to 100 rained down on the city every day. In the next few months, they killed 6,000 people, wounded another 17,000, and damaged or destroyed nearly a million homes and other structures. The toll would have been much worse, but the V-1s weren't very accurate. Some came down in unpopulated areas. Many others were shot down by fighter planes and antiaircraft fire. Eventually U.S. and English bombers knocked out most of the launch sites, though 2,000 airmen died because the sites were heavily defended. Frightened Londoners began breathing easier again.

The respite was brief. A greater threat was in store. Early on the evening of September 8, an enormous explosion rocked a London suburb. The Germans had fired an even more fearsome new weapon, the V-2. This unmanned rocket stood nearly 50 feet high. It soared 50 miles or more into the sky before turning over and heading for its target at nearly 3,500 miles per hour. That was several times the speed of sound, so there was no noise to give advance warning. Even worse, there was no defense against these missiles.

In six months, more than 500 V-2s struck London. Like their predecessor, they were not very accurate. But their much greater speed increased their force at impact and caused more extensive damage. A single rocket could flatten an entire city block. Thousands more people were killed or wounded.

A young British army officer named Arthur C. Clarke was aware of the death and destruction that the V-2s were causing. In later years, he would become a famous science fiction author. He is best known for *2001: A Space Odyssey*, perhaps the most famous science fiction movie ever made. Directed by Stanley Kubrick, the film features a sinister computer named Hal that tries to take over a manned space mission to Jupiter. The film won an Academy Award for special effects in 1968, and Clarke and Kubrick both received Oscar nominations for their work.

Clarke also wrote the novel *Childhood's End*, about invaders from outer space. But they come to Earth to do good. They eliminate war by doing away with individual governments. As a result, world hunger and poverty are also eliminated. Because of Clarke's fame, he was a TV commentator during the first U.S. moon landing expeditions in 1969.

In 1945, long before he had become famous, Clarke had an idea that was anything but science fiction. Even though he was only 27 at the time, he was already a respected member of the British Interplanetary Society and had spent much of World War II working on radar systems.

Like everyone else in London, Clarke was aware of the deadly threat that the V-2 missiles posed. Unlike most of his fellow citizens, however, he saw something in these rockets besides their immediate danger. He thought it might be possible that they could keep going up, rather than turning over and coming down.

It wasn't a new idea. For many years people had dreamed of spaceflight. During the 1860s, French author

Jules Verne published *From the Earth to the Moon* and *Round the Moon*. Those novels suggested that venturing into outer space was possible. Space travel could also come the other way. Englishman H. G. Wells's 1898 novel, *The War of the Worlds*, was about a Martian invasion of Earth. In 1938, an American actor and director named Orson Welles made a Halloween radio broadcast based on the book. A brief announcement at the beginning of the program said that what would follow was fiction. But many people tuned in after the program started and missed the announcement. Welles and the other actors and the sound effects were so realistic that thousands of listeners believed real Martians had landed. Many roads on the East Coast near the site of the "invasion" quickly became packed with panicked motorists trying to escape. Other people armed themselves with shotguns and barricaded themselves in their homes.

Many years before Welles's broadcast, an American named Robert Goddard read Verne's and Wells's books. They helped to convince him that real spaceflight was possible. He launched the first liquid-fueled rocket in 1926. The U.S. government wasn't interested in his invention, but the German government was. The German V-2 used many devices that Goddard had invented. But even with the invention of the V-2, for most people space travel remained in the realm of fiction: either a nightmare or a dream.

Clarke became somewhat of a visionary in February 1945 when he wrote a letter to the editor of *Wireless World*, a British technical magazine. It was titled "Peaceful Uses for V-2" and contained several suggestions. The first was to launch V-2s carrying scientific equipment instead of explosives into the upper atmosphere to send back valuable

Robert Goddard (1882-1945) was an American inventor who was greatly influenced by the works of H.G. Wells and other science fiction writers as a young man. That led him to develop an interest in rockets. He launched the first liquid-fuel rocket in 1926.

information. His second idea was to modify a V-2 to carry a smaller rocket, which would contain a payload with the scientific equipment. This smaller rocket would go fast enough to place its payload into orbit as an "artificial satellite" of Earth. Both these uses could be put into effect within a decade, Clarke believed.

But his third suggestion was the most dramatic. At a certain altitude, an artificial satellite would orbit at exactly the same speed as Earth revolves, making one complete circuit every 24 hours. That would put it in the same relative position with regard to Earth below, in geosynchronous orbit. Three such geosynchronous satellites, spaced 120 degrees apart, would make it possible to provide almost instantaneous television and radio coverage to the entire planet. Because of the curvature of Earth, most electronic signals can only be transmitted for a limited distance. But if they were beamed to a satellite orbiting high overhead, the signal could be returned to receivers thousands of miles away.

Clarke followed up his original letter eight months later with a four-page article titled "Extra-Terrestrial Relays." It made many of the same points and included mathematical calculations as well as detailed diagrams. Because of the enormous technical problems that were involved in building geosynchronous satellites, Clarke anticipated that they would require at least 50 years to become operational.

At first, hardly anyone paid attention to what Clarke had written. When they finally did, Clarke turned out to be partly right. He was correct about establishing communications satellites. He was wrong about the time it would take to build a worldwide network. The first communications satellite was launched only 17 years after his article appeared. Three years later, a geosynchronous satellite went into orbit.

Not long afterward, many people wanted to give the credit to Clarke. They wanted to call him "the father of communications satellites."

Clarke did not want to take the credit. He joked that while he may have been "the godfather" of communications satellites, another man was much more important in actually creating them. This man was an electrical engineer not much older than Clarke. Like Clarke, his imagination had also taken flight when he was a young man. But his preoccupation was primarily with gliders, aircraft that used wind and air currents rather than engines to stay aloft. He began his professional career almost without any guidance or direction. Yet the work he did eventually led to the creation of the modern-day "global village," in which the world seems much smaller than it is because it is possible to see events from virtually any part of the globe on television or on a computer while the events are occurring.

His name is John R. Pierce.

John R. Pierce in later life. As a young man, he was interested
in flying gliders. In addition to his pioneering work with
communications satellites, he was also an author and composer
of computer music.

Chapter 2

A Midwestern Boyhood

John Robinson Pierce was born on March 27, 1910, in Des Moines, Iowa. His parents were Harriet Ann and John Starr Pierce. His mother's maiden name was Robinson, and this became her son's middle name.

Harriet Ann and John Starr Pierce were born and raised in Iowa. John Starr Pierce was a traveling salesman who worked for a milliner, a company that makes women's hats. Harriet, unlike her three sisters, all of whom went to college and became teachers, moved to Des Moines and went to work in a millinery store until her marriage. John Robinson was the couple's only child.

One of John's earliest memories was of a visit to his grandfather in Cedar Falls that lasted for several months. The trip itself would have been an adventure, as the town was nearly a hundred miles from Des Moines over primitive roads. The Cedar Falls property included a barn with a horse and buggy, details the youngster would remember the rest of his life.

Not long afterward, the family moved to St. Paul, Minnesota, the first of several moves that John would make while he was growing up. Because of his job, John's father was away from home quite often.

"I was really my mother's child," he recalled in a 1992 interview with Andrew Goldstein of the Institute of Electrical and Electronics Engineers (IEEE). "My father was a good man. He was a quiet man, not brilliant, not dumb. My mother had a sharper mind than he did."

When John was six years old, he started school. His first classroom was in a small portable building with outside plumbing. From the beginning, he was an excellent student. It was also clear what he most liked to do.

"I was always interested in things of a technical nature, whether Mechano sets, or my American Model Builder, or toy steam engines, or electric motors," he explained in a 1979 interview with Harriett Lyle. "I regarded electric motors as a sort of natural magic and got my mother to read me things about them. I tried to learn, but without much understanding. I suppose that science looked to me like the magic of the day. If you wanted to do great things, you didn't ride on broomsticks; you invoked the mysterious forces of science."

Even though neither of his parents had any scientific or technical background, they encouraged John in this interest. And this interest really took off when he learned how to read on his own.

As Calvin Tomkins wrote in a 1963 article in *New Yorker* magazine, "As soon as he learned to read himself, he devoured scientific literature of all kinds, good and bad. 'There were fewer good books on science then,' he [John] said recently, 'and fewer teachers who knew anything about it. I read all the popular-science magazines, and I was fascinated by science fiction.'"

Like Robert Goddard, John was especially interested in reading books by such famous science fiction authors as Jules Verne and H. G. Wells. It was an interest that would stay with him for the rest of his life.

The youngster also enjoyed working with his hands. He had an early fascination with radios and other technical gadgets, even building several primitive radios. He described himself as a "tinkerer," a person who enjoys playing around with mechanical things.

"Tinkering was a part of youthful activities in those days," he explained to Andrew Goldstein. "There were lots of things around. I often wonder how children are ever exposed to anything that really works these days. In those days there were still blacksmith shops, there were machine shops. People still lived in towns rather than in suburbs, and there were all sorts of technical activities going on within walking distance. You walked right past them. You learn with your hands, not your head."

When John was about 12, his father quit his sales job. He went into the millinery business in partnership with his brother. They owned several stores, one of which was in Mason City, Iowa. It was just south of the Minnesota border and about halfway between St. Paul and Des Moines.

John finished elementary school in Mason City and went to high school there for two years. While he continued to do well in all his subjects, he especially enjoyed mathematics, chemistry, and physics. Because of all the reading that he did, he also liked English.

The family moved back to St. Paul for a year and John had to change schools for his junior year in high school. He probably had an inspiring English teacher because he began writing poetry at that time. Then his father retired from the millinery business. The Pierces left their solid Midwest heritage behind and moved to Long Beach, California, where John enrolled in Woodrow Wilson High School. It wouldn't take long for the young man to leave the solid Earth behind.

John R. Pierce is shown taking off in the first glider that he built with friends. The towrope, which several people are pulling to give the aircraft enough speed to become airborne, is visible at the right side of the picture. Note his exposed position in the front of the glider. At that time, no one thought of wearing any kind of head protection.

Chapter 3
Taking Flight

While he was attending Woodrow Wilson, John read an article in *National Geographic* entitled "On the Wings of the Wind." It was about gliding in Germany. The Treaty of Versailles, which ended World War I, imposed harsh economic and military restrictions on Germany. During the war, German fighter planes such as the one piloted by Baron Manfred von Richthofen (the legendary Red Baron, who shot down more than 80 Allied aircraft before being killed himself at the age of 25) had done a great deal of damage. One restriction was that Germany could no longer build aircraft with engines. German pilots turned to gliding in graceful sailplanes, which didn't need engines to stay aloft.

"What teen-ager would not thrill to the pictures of beautiful and strangely shaped sailplanes soaring over romantic countrysides?" John wrote in an article titled "The Wings of the Wind." "How romantic, too, were the foreign names: the universities of Aachen and Darmstadt, where the students had formed clubs to build and fly gliders. How much I would have given to have flown for hours and to have covered tens and hundreds of miles."

There was only one solution: John had to build his own glider. With the aid of two school friends, Oliver La Rue and Apollo Smith, he set to work. The "hangar" was Apollo's garage, with Apollo's father, sisters, and younger brother looking on.

"The glider which we built in Apollo's garage was conceived in ignorance and begot of bicycle spokes for turnbuckles, wagon wheels, piano wire and fancy," he wrote in "The Wings of the Wind." "The airfoil was laid out by Oliver La Rue with freehand sweeps. At a moderate pace, the rickety monstrosity grew."

Finally it was ready. The boys wheeled it to the top of a nearby hill. Apollo climbed into the pilot's seat. That required a certain amount of courage because the glider was open-framed: there was nothing but air between the seat and the ground. The rest of the onlookers attached a rope to the glider's nose and began running downhill against the wind. The glider rose briefly into the air.

Then it crashed.

Fortunately Apollo wasn't hurt, and the boys quickly figured out the problem. The struts that supported the wing needed to be stronger. When they tried again, Oliver's airfoil worked perfectly.

The boys weren't the only ones interested in gliders. There was a glider club at a nearby airport. The boys soaked up knowledge from other men who were working on gliders. They learned to improve their flying skills. They competed in a glider competition in San Diego during the summer and won several events.

Just before the competition, John graduated at the top of his class from Woodrow Wilson High School. Now he had to decide what to do with his life. Though neither of his parents had gone to college, they wanted their son to continue his education. So did John. Because they hadn't lived in California very long, they didn't know much about the schools there. Almost by accident, John learned about the California Institute of Technology, more familiarly known as Caltech. It was in Pasadena, not far from his home in

Long Beach, and seemed to fit the courses that he'd enjoyed in high school. He took the entrance examination and passed.

"He was feeling, as he puts it, 'full of knowledge,' and in this condition he was approached by Hugo Gernsback, an early publisher of popular-science journals and of the world's first science-fiction magazine," wrote Calvin Tomkins. "Gernsback proposed that Pierce write a book about gliding. John agreed, and the result appeared late in 1929 as *How to Build and Fly Gliders,* priced at one dollar a copy."

There was no doubt that the book was widely read. People constantly wrote to John, asking him for plans. He even got a package from Australia. A man sent a sample of local wood, asking if it would be suitable for building a glider.

In later life, John thought about this first literary effort. In "The Wings of the Wind" he wrote, "I have often wondered whether this book, together with other articles I wrote for Gernsback's magazines, did real harm. Because of me, did human beings build crazy gliders without benefit of engineering, and kill themselves therewith? I wouldn't be a bit surprised."

But he concluded that if he hadn't written the book, someone else might have. And that other person might have done an even worse job. "Truthfully," he concluded, "the only guilt I feel concerning *How to Build and Fly Gliders* is the atrocious English in which it is written. At that age, I couldn't be expected to know about gliders, but I should have known how to express myself better."

After he entered Caltech, John continued to fly. He built a larger glider that could hold a passenger as well as the pilot. His mother even went up with him on one occasion.

Then he built a sailplane. It was fully enclosed and had a wingspan of 45 feet. That made it much larger than the earlier gliders. In addition, it had controls, so it could be taken on longer flights. The boys took their craft to the Palos Verdes Peninsula. It had a high hill that overlooked the Pacific Ocean. Today it is covered with expensive homes, but back then it was almost deserted.

"One clear, fine day, when the wind blew strongly from the ocean, I flew out over the dune and turned left. The wind lifted me up, and when I came to the end of the dune I turned out into the wind, clear around and back over the dune again. I was soaring, and learning more than I had in months before. The wind was whistling past me. I pulled back and flew higher still. This was all that I had been waiting for. There was the dune. There was the blue sea. There was the hill and the crowd. I saw flashes of each, and all the time there was I, hundreds of feet in the air, turning, rising, turning, rising, learning to fly my sailplane in an endless series of figure eights," he wrote in "The Wings of the Wind."

But there was another side to gliding. What goes up must come down. Sometimes very hard. Moments after John landed on that memorable day, another sailplane crashed nearby. The pilot, a good friend of John's, died from his injuries as dozens of people looked on in horror. Soon four more people he knew were killed in gliding accidents. A member of the gliding club joked to him that there was a bulletin board with newspaper clippings about everyone who had died. The member added that they were saving a place for John as well.

"By this time I was scared," John wrote in "The Wings of the Wind." "I sold my gliders and built a fourteen-foot boat out of quarter-inch plywood, in which I went sailing on the ocean. I flew a few times more, when someone invited me. And, to this day, when I look down a fine slope, over fields and houses, with the wind in my face, I long for wings. I long to soar out over it all."

Though John R. Pierce had no knowledge of vacuum tubes when he began working for Bell Laboratories, he learned quickly. His research led to the development of dozens of patents for Bell.

Chapter 4
Beginning with Bell Laboratories

John's flying days may have ended, but his college days had just begun.

At first he thought he would major in chemistry. One reason was that he was interested in photography. He often took pictures of the gliders he'd built. Developing the film involved several chemicals. John thought that he might eventually work for the Eastman Kodak Company, at that time the leading producer of photographic film. In addition, Orsino Smith, Apollo's father, was a chemical engineer.

But that idea quickly faded. Even though he had done well in chemistry in high school, he had trouble understanding the lectures at Caltech. Even worse, his experiments were all disasters. He kept dropping equipment and spilling chemicals. He was fortunate that he didn't injure himself.

Because of his interest in gliders, he next considered aeronautical engineering. The work involved designing airplanes. Again he ran into problems.

"I got awfully tired of drawing rivets, and began looking for a field with no rivets in it," he told Calvin Tomkins. "What I settled on finally was electrical engineering."

He didn't spend all his time at Caltech going to class and reading books. John worked on the student newspaper and other Caltech publications. He wrote several stories for Hugo Gernsback. He also enjoyed hiking. One time he went on a long camping trip with some friends in Yosemite

National Park, several hundred miles north of Pasadena. Perhaps most important for his future career, he entered a science fiction writing contest. His story won second place.

He received his bachelor of science degree in electrical engineering in 1933. The nation was in the midst of the Great Depression and few jobs were available. With his parents continuing to pay his tuition, he earned his master's degree the following year and his Ph.D. in 1936.

"I really didn't know where I was going," he told Harriett Lyle decades later. "I didn't know what the world was like. Those were the days of the Depression—very different from this."

With so many people desperately looking for work, John was lucky. One of his professors helped get him a job with Bell Laboratories. Bell Laboratories was the research arm of the American Telephone and Telegraph Company (now called AT&T), which at that time had a virtual monopoly on telephone service in the United States.

As a graduation present for earning his Ph.D., his parents gave him a trip to Europe before he started his new job. He bicycled around England, then traveled through much of the European continent by train. When he returned to the United States, he rode a train across the country to see his mother and father and to collect a few items, then once again crossed the continent to New York.

"I was glad to have a job," he explained to Harriett Lyle. "I'd always lived with my parents to save money. They had moved to Pasadena when I went to school at Caltech, and I was glad to get away. I was glad to go to New York, which sounded glamorous in those days. It was an entirely fresh start in life."

He didn't realize just how fresh it would be. He was quickly put to work doing research on vacuum tubes. Invented about 20 years earlier, vacuum tubes were especially important in the steadily growing telephone business. The tubes were glass bulbs that contained electrical wiring. Because all the air was pumped out, the electrical current could be precisely controlled. That was important because telephone signals weakened as they traveled along telephone lines. By boosting the amount of electrical current, the telephone signals could be amplified, or increased in strength. With a network of vacuum-tube repeaters set up all over the country, long-distance telephoning became possible.

For John, the job involved one huge problem. As he told Harriett Lyle, "That [the vacuum tube] is one thing that I'd never thought of before going to Bell Laboratories. I can hardly think of a thing that I knew less about."

The company wasn't much help at first. They didn't provide him with specific directions for his work.

There was a reason for this. As Calvin Tomkins explains, some Bell Laboratories researchers such as John were "encouraged to engage in 'unprogrammed and unscheduled work,' the sole proviso being that the research be related in some way to the field of electrical communication—a field that takes in so many aspects of scientific activity that its boundaries are hard to define. This policy has paid spectacular dividends from the very beginning."

Despite the freedom that he was given, it was hard for John to feel that he was doing anything useful. Being left to himself was somewhat confusing.

As he told Calvin Tomkins, "In those days, unless you had a reputation, you did what they told you to do. My first years were rather unproductive. I was slow in getting a grip on things. But gradually I learned how to bring the results of study to bear on problems, and then I made a few inventions."

John was being modest. These "few inventions" resulted in dozens of patents for Bell Laboratories. He soon had a reputation as one of the brightest young minds in the company. After World War II began, his research became even more focused. He did work for the U.S. military that contributed to the development of radar.

During this period, he continued to write science fiction. He also wrote a number of scientific essays. He adopted the pen name of J.J. Coupling, a term used in electrical engineering. That helped him to avoid strict rules that Bell Laboratories had for articles written by employees.

World War II ended in 1945. Two years later, three of John's colleagues at Bell Laboratories—William Shockley, Walter Brattain, and John Bardeen—invented a device that would eventually replace the cumbersome vacuum tube. It was smaller, used less energy, and provided more accurate control over the electrical current. Nine years later the device would earn the three men a Nobel prize. But at the time, they didn't have a name for their invention. Because of John's experience as a writer, they thought that he could come up with something.

John thought about what the new device would do. It transferred electrical signals across a resistor, a device that's used to help control electrical current. He also thought that the name should be similar to those of other electrical devices, such as *varistor* and *thermistor.*

He called the Nobel-winning device the transistor.

Inventing the name for the device that would revolutionize modern-day electronics would prove to be just one of his accomplishments. Something far greater was in store.

In 1949, John tests a model of a traveling wave tube, one of several Bell Laboratories developments that made satellite communications possible.

The coronation of Queen Elizabeth II of England in 1953 was an event that attracted worldwide attention. Film of the colorful ceremony was rushed to jet bombers of the Royal Air Force, which flew it across the Atlantic. People in the United States and Canada saw the film on their televisions that evening.

Chapter 5

The Birth of an Idea

While V-2 rockets had spread fear among London residents during World War II, they were regarded in a different way now that the war was over and the danger had passed. Many V-2 scientists came to the United States. They brought unused rockets with them to help in research. Some of the rockets were equipped with cameras to take pictures of Earth and of objects in space.

When these pictures were published, many people became interested in the possibility of space travel. Because of his science fiction stories and his status as an engineer doing cutting edge research at Bell Laboratories, John was often invited to give public lectures on spaceflight.

"The subject of these talks was the sort of man-in-space romanticization common in science fiction magazines," he said in an article entitled "*Echo*—America's First Communications Satellite." "The talks were fun, and audiences enjoyed them."

The talks may also have stimulated John's imagination and started him thinking about the same questions that Arthur C. Clarke had raised a few years earlier. Even though John wasn't aware of Clarke's writing in *Wireless World,* he wrote an article called "Don't Write: Telegraph." It appeared in the March 1952 issue of *Astounding Science Fiction.* Despite the magazine's title, there was nothing make-believe about the ideas that John put forth.

He began the article this way: "Perhaps readers would like to know the facts about interplanetary communication:

why it is easy by very standard methods at a time when even the Moon rocket is largely wishful thinking."

He started by discussing the problems of long-distance communication on Earth. He explained that both wires and short-wave radios were impractical. Wires were cumbersome and expensive and required frequent amplifiers. Short-wave radio signals were cheaper and could span long distances but depended on the right atmospheric conditions. In addition, the existing short-wave frequencies were very crowded.

Because of his research at Bell Laboratories, John was aware of a third alternative: microwaves. While they are well-known for their use in small ovens that quickly cook and heat food, they are actually very short radio waves. John knew that they could carry a great deal of information. But they had one significant disadvantage. They could only be transmitted in a straight line. Because of Earth's curvature, their maximum "line of sight" transmission distance was only about 30 miles. That meant that coast-to-coast transmissions would involve more than 100 repeater stations. Those would be very expensive.

John had a solution. Like Clarke, he too looked upward. Microwave signals had no problem penetrating Earth's atmosphere. He made several mathematical calculations and concluded that microwave signals could reach nearby stars without using much power.

Shortly before "Don't Write: Telegraph" was published, 26-year-old Princess Elizabeth became Queen of England. Her coronation, which occurred some 16 months later on June 2, 1953, was considered an especially significant event.

Television cameras recorded every moment of the solemn occasion. Millions of viewers crowded around television sets in England to watch the ceremonies live. Millions of other viewers in countries around the world also crowded around their sets. But very few of them saw it live.

Film of the elaborate ceremony was taken to a London airport and loaded onto Canberra jet bombers of the Royal Air Force. The planes took off and flew to the United States and Canada. When they landed, the film was rushed to television stations in those countries. Soon millions of parents called their children inside on a warm evening to watch the coronation. They considered it almost miraculous that this important event could be witnessed thousands of miles away, just six or seven hours after it had taken place.

Soon afterward, John began taking the first steps that would eventually allow events such as Queen Elizabeth's coronation to be seen instantaneously, no matter how far away the viewers were located from the actual scene. His invention would do away with fleets of jet bombers and delays of several hours. In 1954 he was invited to give a talk to the annual meeting of the Institute of Radio Engineers. He had a great deal of respect for the organization. His usual lectures on science fiction did not seem appropriate for such a highly professional group.

"What could I speak of? The idea of communication satellites came to me. I didn't think of this as my idea, it was just in the air," he explained in "*Echo.*"

"It was easy for me to calculate the power needed to send signals from one place on the surface of the earth to another by means of a communication satellite," he continued. "I was amazed and delighted at the outcome of my calculations. By using currently available microwave equipment, any of these sorts of satellites could be used to communicate across oceans."

He discussed two possible types of satellites. One would be an active repeater, the other would be a passive reflector.

An active repeater would receive signals sent from Earth. It would amplify them and then send them on to another station, hundreds and even thousands of miles away from the station that had originally sent the signals. That would eliminate the necessity for costly relay stations. But there was one major disadvantage. An active repeater satellite would require its own source of power. Since no appropriate power source at that time had more than a limited lifetime (sort of like non-rechargeable batteries), active repeaters weren't practical from a financial standpoint. It would cost millions of dollars to build them and then launch them into orbit. Yet they would transmit for only a limited amount of time and then go silent.

Passive reflectors avoided that problem. They would simply reflect the signals to Earth, though some of the signal strength would be lost. The best type of reflector, John said, would be a sphere about 100 feet in diameter. It would be covered in aluminum foil and placed in orbit about 1,000 miles above Earth.

The audience enjoyed his speech. Several listeners urged him to make a written presentation. Called "Orbital Radio Relays," the article appeared the following April in *Jet Propulsion,* a journal published by the American Rocket

Society. This time he raised other concerns. One was that electronic equipment that functioned reliably on Earth might not work so well in the harsh conditions that existed hundreds of miles overhead. The main problem, however, was that the U.S. government wasn't particularly interested in doing anything like that. It appeared that John's idea would never get off the ground.

Then, on an autumn day in 1957, an object not much larger than a basketball changed everything.

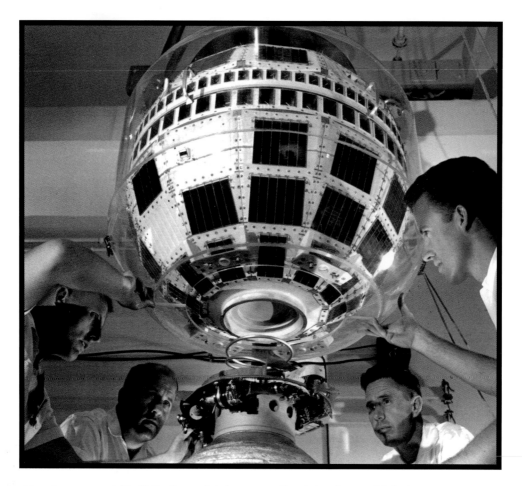

Engineers at Bell Laboratories conduct tests on Telstar. Launched in 1962, it was the first active repeater communications satellite. It allowed people to watch live television transmissions from several thousand miles away.

Chapter 6

Into Space!

The Soviet Union launched *Sputnik* into orbit around Earth on October 4, 1957. Millions of people went out at night to look up at what was the first artificial Earth satellite. Even though it was less than two feet in diameter and weighed less than 200 pounds, sharp-eyed viewers could spot the glowing trail it created as it raced across the dark skies hundreds of miles above them.

The Soviets launched *Sputnik 2* less than a month later. It was much larger than its predecessor, weighing more than half a ton. Even more impressive, it had a passenger: a dog named Laika, which is Russian for "barker." Unfortunately, there was no way to bring the spacecraft back to Earth, and Laika soon died.

A sense of near panic gripped the United States. The country was frantic to catch up. If the Soviet Union could launch a satellite into space, perhaps they could also launch guided missiles with nuclear warheads at this country. Many people believed that our educational system had failed. Politicians and the public demanded that schools start crash programs in science.

These demands only increased when there was another type of crash. With a great deal of publicity, the U.S. Navy's Vanguard rocket was launched from Cape Canaveral in Florida on December 6, 1957. Carrying a small satellite, it rose a few feet, then collapsed and burst into flames. It was humiliating. One newspaper headline read, "Oh, What a Flopnik!"

Fortunately, the U.S. Army had produced another kind of rocket, the Jupiter-C. It was successfully launched a few weeks later, on January 31. It carried *Explorer 1*, the country's first Earth satellite, into orbit. Even though it was much smaller than *Sputnik 1*, the whole nation breathed a little easier. From a scientific viewpoint, *Explorer 1* was a much greater accomplishment than *Sputnik*. It discovered the Van Allen radiation belt that circles Earth. *Sputnik 1* did little more than beep, which allowed Soviet ground stations to track its progress.

One of the first consequences of the Soviet launch was the creation of the Advanced Research Projects Agency, also known as ARPA. While ARPA would eventually lead the way in creating the Internet, its immediate concern was to prevent any more nasty surprises by insuring American technological superiority. Another consequence was the creation of the National Aeronautics and Space Administration (NASA) to coordinate all nonmilitary space projects. A third was an opportunity for John Pierce and his colleagues.

In 1958 John saw pictures of a balloon that NASA scientist William J. O'Sullivan had constructed to measure the density of the air at an altitude of one thousand miles. The balloon stood a hundred feet high and was made of plastic covered with metal.

"That was just what I was thinking about for communication," John told Harriett Lyle. "Then the problem was getting it launched. We went around to all the different agencies—the Air Force and ARPA. They were all interested in much more ambitious things." Even some important Bell executives opposed the project.

Early in 1959, attitudes changed. Bell Laboratories decided to support the project. And NASA agreed to launch the satellite.

With the two *Sputnik*s circling Earth every hour and a half, the scientific community began to move quickly. The Jet Propulsion Laboratory (JPL) had previously built two ground stations for other purposes. These would be capable of tracking signals from the proposed satellite. Rudolph Kompfner, a colleague of John's at Bell Laboratories, squeezed the company's budget and funded an antenna in New Jersey that could receive messages from space.

But a problem soon cropped up. The balloon was far too large to fit into any rocket. It would have to be folded flat, then inflated in space. There would be tremendous pressure as the balloon expanded rapidly in what was almost a complete vacuum. And it couldn't be made in one piece. The balloon consisted of 82 separate panels that were glued together. The first test, conducted in October 1959, was a disaster. The glue couldn't hold the panels together when the balloon began to inflate. It quickly disintegrated and made a spectacular light show over the East Coast of the United States.

A new, stronger adhesive material was developed. In a test launch on April Fools Day in 1960, everything worked perfectly. NASA made plans for a full orbital launch the following month. This time the rocket failed. It plunged into the Atlantic Ocean.

A few months later, everything came together.

"The Thor-Delta performed flawlessly, lifting the payload on the morning of 12 August 1960 to the desired altitude," Donald Elder wrote in "Something of Value: *Echo* and the Beginnings of Satellite Communications." "The ejection mechanism in the final stage sent the tightly folded collapsed sphere into the near vacuum of Earth's orbit; then a combination of chemicals inside the balloon underwent a process of sublimation of released gas that gently inflated the sphere. The satellite—at that point officially named *Echo*—had achieved orbit."

Two ground stations soon located the satellite in orbit. One of the JPL stations transmitted a short prerecorded message from President Dwight D. Eisenhower. Moments later, John and other elated Bell Laboratories scientists in New Jersey clearly heard the president's distinctive voice.

The satellite worked.

There would be more accomplishments over the next few days. JPL and Bell Laboratories had a successful two-way transmission. Then came a three-way signal. Soon afterward, the satellite was used to transmit pictures.

With the success of *Echo,* Bell was willing to spend much more money on communications satellites. Even before *Echo* went into orbit, John had become interested in active repeater satellites. Now he was authorized to begin building one, which was named *Telstar.* Another division of Bell Laboratories had solved the power problem by designing solar cells. About 3,600 solar cells were used in the satellite, a sphere about three feet in diameter. It weighed 175 pounds.

Telstar was launched from Cape Canaveral, Florida, on July 10, 1962. The following day millions of television viewers around the country saw an image of the U.S. flag being broadcast live from a station in Maine. Moments later they saw images of other flags flying in France and in England.

The new satellite created a sensation. The Tornadoes, a British rock group, recorded a song called "Telstar." The song spent a total of 13 weeks on the Billboard Top 40 chart, three of them in the number one spot. Jazz great Duke Ellington composed a piece that he also called "Telstar."

For John Pierce, the sky was no longer the limit. The limit came from something much more earthbound: the U.S. Congress.

Soon after *Telstar*'s successful debut, Congress passed the Communications Satellite Act. According to the act, international satellite communications had to be routed through a new company known as COMSAT (Communications Satellite Corporation), which would have a monopoly. That took Bell Laboratories and John R. Pierce out of the communications satellite business.

"I took that hard, you know," he told Andrew Goldstein. "I'd just got into satellites, communication satellites, and covered my name with glory—deserved or not deserved. I felt thrust out into the cold."

John Pierce's pioneering work in communications satellites was finished. But his career was hardly through.

John continued his successful activities at Bell Laboratories for several more years. Bell Laboratories had a mandatory retirement age of 65, yet John was hardly ready to stop working. He wanted to stay active. In 1971, when he was 61, Caltech offered him the opportunity to become a professor of engineering there. John jumped at the chance and once again crossed the country. In 1979 he became chief technologist at the nearby Jet Propulsion Laboratory, a position he held for three years.

By the time he was well past the age at which most people are content to retire, John was ready to take on still another challenge. In 1983 he moved to Stanford University in Palo Alto, California, where he became associated with the school's Center for Computer Research in Music and Acoustics. He had long been interested in music, having taken piano lessons during his childhood and continuing to play at Caltech.

As he explained in his book *The Science of Musical Sound*, "The study of musical sound is important only because music is important, and because the quality of sound is important to music. Some thirty years ago at Bell Laboratories, all the research on speech and hearing was moved into my division. My reaction to this encounter with the science of sound was love at first sight."

John was able to maintain this love despite the demands of producing the first communications satellites. Soon after the launching of *Telstar*, one of his Bell Laboratories colleagues discovered a way of making a computer produce musical sounds that couldn't be created in any other way. John immediatcly bccame interested.

"Ever since I first tinkered with computer-produced sounds, such sounds, and particularly musical sounds, have been closest to my heart," he explained in *The Science of Musical Sound*. He even composed computer music for two Decca records.

Although he was officially a visiting professor of music at Stanford, his "visit" lasted for well over a decade. During that time he helped raise millions of dollars to put the center on a firm financial footing. Yet he refused to accept any money for his teaching.

By then, he could look back on 20 books of which he was the author or coauthor, 90 patents, 300 scientific papers, and two dozen science fiction stories.

He summed up his life's work in "*Echo.*" "My work on communication satellites brought me more public recognition than anything else that I have done," he wrote. "Communication satellites are very important as technological tools of communication. They have brought into our homes events from all parts of the world—Olympic Games, a coronation, a royal wedding. When the old dream of a journey to the moon was realized, something entirely new, communications satellites, sent pictures of the triumphant astronauts to all nations. Alas, satellites show us disasters, famines and wars in far lands, that have a worldwide impact because we see them.

"In the sparsely settled part of Massachusetts where I am writing these words, a considerable number of homes have microwave dishes that point at the satellites which distribute TV programs around the country, and these dishes pick up tens of channels intended for broadcast and cable distribution. A few weeks ago I returned from a cruise on the Greek ship *Illyria.* The ship had a satellite terminal, and one could, and some did, use it to make calls back to the United States. A broker kept in touch with his firm; a mother with her children. I could go on almost endlessly about the impact of communication satellites."

That impact earned him a great deal of recognition. He was awarded a prestigious Marconi International

Fellowship by Columbia University, the National Medal of Science, and the IEEE Medal of Honor. He also received honorary doctorate degrees from many of the country's most famous universities, such as Yale, Columbia, and Northwestern.

In 1985 he was awarded the Japan Prize. It included 50 million yen in cash, or nearly $200,000. Ten years later he and Harold Rosen, who took communications satellites one step further by designing the first geosynchronous satellite, shared the Charles Stark Draper Prize, one of the highest honors in the field of engineering. Like the earlier award, it earned John $200,000.

John R. Pierce died of pneumonia on April 2, 2002. By that time advances in telecommunications had left him behind. Yet none of these advances diminished his acknowledged title as the father of the telecommunications industry. A press release on the 40th anniversary of the *Telstar* launch pointed out, "*Telstar* demonstrated the feasibility of using satellites to provide voice, data and video communications between continents, which was a giant leap forward in the creation of the global communications village we enjoy today. It erased any distinctions between phoning around the corner and phoning around the world, in terms of the speed and quality of the connection. It also ushered in the era of transcontinental television transmission, adding the phrase 'live via satellite' to the common vernacular."

As writer Donald Elder points out, even more basically, "It is important to remember that a successful communications satellite effort, however simple in design and execution, was necessary for individuals to plan a more ambitious generation of devices. The telecommunications industry today may be 'the world's largest economic sector,' as the *Los Angeles Times* has proclaimed, but few companies would have allocated resources for a field that had yielded no apparent hope of success until August 1960. Viewing the results yielded by *Echo*, individuals could envision more ambitious telecommunications projects for the future.

"*Echo*, then, represents the proverbial first step in a journey in which the world is still participating today."

John R. Pierce Chronology

1910 Born on March 27 in Des Moines, Iowa

1927 Moves to California

1928 Graduates from high school; builds his first glider

1929 Publishes *How to Build and Fly Gliders*

1933 Receives bachelor of science degree from Caltech

1934 Receives master of science degree from Caltech

1936 Receives Ph.D. from Caltech; travels in Europe; begins working at Bell Labs

1949 Coins the word *transistor* for new device invented by colleagues at Bell Laboratories

1952 His article "Don't Write: Telegraph" is published in *Astounding Science Fiction* magazine

1954 Delivers address about communications satellites to annual meeting of the Institute of Radio Engineers

1955 Publishes article about communications satellites in *Jet Propulsion* magazine

1960 Launch of *Echo*

1962 Launch of *Telstar*

1971 Retires from Bell Laboratories; begins teaching at Caltech

1979 Receives Marconi International Fellowship

1983 Begins teaching computer music at Stanford University

1985 Receives the Japan Prize

1995 Receives the Charles Stark Draper Prize

2002 Dies on April 2

Timeline of Discovery

1876 Alexander Graham Bell patents the telephone.

1878 The first telephone directory, listing fifty names, is printed in Hartford, Connecticut.

1889 William Gray invents the public pay telephone.

1910 Nearly 6 million Americans subscribe to telephone service.

1915 Alexander Graham Bell makes first transcontinental telephone call.

1926 Robert Goddard launches the first successful liquid-fueled rocket.

1935 The first round-the-world telephone call is made from one office to another office in the same building.

1938 Orson Welles makes *War of the Worlds* radio broadcast.

1939 World War II begins.

1941 United States enters World War II after the Japanese bomb Pearl Harbor, Hawaii.

1945 Arthur C. Clarke publishes letter to the editor and article in *Wireless World* about communications satellites; World War II ends.

1952 Telephone area codes are introduced.

1957 Soviet Union launches *Sputnik,* the first artificial Earth satellite.

1958 U.S. Army launches first U.S. Earth satellite, *Explorer 1.*

1961 Soviet cosmonaut Yuri Gagarin becomes the first human in space.

1962 U.S. Congress passes Communications Satellite Act.

1963 Designed by Harold Rosen, *Syncom 2* becomes the first communications satellite to achieve geosynchronous orbit.

1969 U.S. astronaut Neil Armstrong becomes the first human to set foot on the surface of the moon.

1973 Motorola Corporation executive Martin Cooper invents the cellular telephone.

1981 U.S. space shuttle *Columbia* makes its first flight.

1983 Mobile wireless telephone service begins.

1988 Sprint begins first nationwide fiber optic telephone service.

1990 Tim Berners-Lee develops software that leads to creation of the World Wide Web.

1996 U.S. Congress passes the Telecommunications Act, which deregulates telephone service and increases competition.

2002 The number of cell phone subscribers in the Unites States passes 130 million.

2003 As a standard feature on high-end models, major automobile manufacturers begin including technological devices such as OnStar, which uses the Global Positioning System (GPS) satellite network to provide information, safety, and security services.

Further Reading

For Young Adults

Bankston, John. *Robert Goddard and the Liquid Rocket Engine.* Bear, DE: Mitchell Lane Publishers, 2002.

Fields, Alice. *Satellites.* New York: Franklin Watts, 1981.

Gaines, Ann. *Tim Berners-Lee and the Development of the World Wide Web.* Bear, DE: Mitchell Lane Publishers, 2002.

Parker, Steve. *Satellites.* Austin, TX: Raintree Steck-Vaughn, 1997.

Stevenson, John. *Visual Science: Telecommunications.* Morristown, NJ: Silver Burdett Company, 1985.

Walker, Niki. *Satellites and Space Probes.* New York: Crabtree Publishing Company, 1998.

Webb, Marcus. *Telephones: Words Over Wires.* San Diego, CA: Lucent Books, Inc., 1992.

Works Consulted

—"40 Years of *Telstar.*" http://www.lucent.com/minds/telstar/fit.html

—"John Pierce, Bell Labs Scientist: Man Who Named the Transistor Dies at 92" http://www.bell-labs.com/news/2002/april/pierce.html

Elder, Donald C. "Something of Value: *Echo* and the Beginnings of Satellite Communications." http://history.nasa.gov/SP-4217/ch4.htm

Goldstein, Andrew. "John R. Pierce, Electrical Engineer," an oral history conducted in 1992 by Andrew Goldstein, IEEE History Center, Rutgers University, New Brunswick, NJ, USA. „ 1992.

Lyle, Harriett. Interview with John R. Pierce. California Institute of Technology Oral History Project. 1982 by the California Institute of Technology.

Pierce, John R. "Don't Write: Telegraph." *Science, Art, and Communication.* New York: Clarkson N. Potter, Inc., 1968.

Pierce, John R. "*Echo*—America's First Communications Satellite." http://www.smecc.org/John_Pierce___echoredo.htm. Southwest Museum of Engineering, Communications and Computation.

Pierce, John R. *The Science of Musical Sound.* New York: Scientific American Books, 1983.

Pierce, John R. "*Telstar,* a History." http://www.smecc.org/John_Pierce1.htm. Southwest Museum of Engineering, Communications and Computation.

Pierce, John R. "The Wings of the Wind." *Science, Art, and Communication.* New York: Clarkson N. Potter, Inc., 1968.

Pierce, John R., and A. Michael Noll. *Signals: The Science of Telecommunications.* New York: Scientific American Library, 1990.

Tomkins, Calvin. "Woomera Has It!" *New Yorker,* September 21, 1963.

Index